K is for Kwanzaa
A Kwanzaa Alphabet Book

by JUWANDA G. FORD

Illustrated by KEN WILSON-MAX

Cartwheel
·B·O·O·K·S·®

SCHOLASTIC INC.
New York Toronto London Auckland Sydney

For my
sister
Joszette,
who loves to celebrate everything!
—J.G.F.

To my
cousin
Amber,
who needs no excuse to have fun!
—K.W.M.

Text copyright © 1997 by Juwanda G. Ford.
Illustrations copyright © 1997 by Ken Wilson-Max.
All rights reserved. Published by Scholastic Inc.
CARTWHEEL BOOKS and the CARTWHEEL BOOKS logo
are trademarks and/or registered trademarks of Scholastic Inc.

Library of Congress Cataloging-in-Publication Data

Ford, Juwanda G.
    K is for Kwanzaa : a Kwanzaa alphabet book / by Juwanda G. Ford ; illustrated by
Ken Wilson-Max.
       p.   cm.
    Summary: Celebrates the African-American holiday Kwanzaa by introducing related
words from A to Z, including "Africa," "bendera," "dashiki," and "yams."
    ISBN 0-590-92200-9 (alk. paper)
    1. Kwanzaa—Juvenile literature. 2. Afro-Americans—Social life and customs—
Juvenile literature. 3. Alphabets—Juvenile literature. [1. Kwanzaa. 2. Afro-Americans—
Social life and customs. 3. Alphabet.] I. Wilson-Max, Ken, ill. II. Title.
GT4403.F67   1997
394.261—dc21   96-51728
                                                                                 CIP
                                                                                 AC

10 9 8 7 6 5 4 3 2 1

Printed in Singapore   46
First printing, November 1997

Kwanzaa (KWAN-zah) is a non-religious holiday that honors African-American people and their heritage. *Everyone* can join in the Kwanzaa celebration, which lasts for seven days from December 26 until January 1.

Kwanzaa was started in 1966 by Dr. Maulana Karenga, an African-American teacher. He wanted to help African Americans learn about their African history, culture, and customs.

Dr. Karenga took the name for the holiday from the Swahili word "Kwanza," which means "the first fruits of the harvest." The extra "a" was added so the name would have seven letters to match the seven principles of Kwanzaa. First harvest, when crops are gathered, is a time of great celebration in many regions of Africa. Like first harvest, Kwanzaa is an exciting and joyful occasion.

Let's celebrate Kwanzaa from A to Z!

The Seven Kwanzaa Principles

The seven principles of Kwanzaa are called Nguzo Saba (en-GOO-zoh SAH-bah). There is a different principle for each of the seven days. The principles are used to guide us through the Kwanzaa celebration and to help us think about the meaning of Kwanzaa. Although these principles are studied during this holiday season, we can continue to practice them every day.

Umoja (oo-MOH-jah) — unity
Umoja is celebrated on the first day of Kwanzaa. Unity means living together peacefully as a family and community.

Kujichagulia (koo-JEE-chah-goo-LEE-ah) — self-determination
Self-determination is deciding what we want and making goals for ourselves. This is practiced on the second day.

Ujima (oo-JEE-mah) — collective work and responsibility
Ujima is celebrated on the third day. Ujima means working together as a community to solve problems and take care of our neighborhood.

Ujamaa (oo-jah-MAH) — cooperative economics
On the fourth day, Ujamaa is studied. This principle teaches the value of owning and operating our own businesses.

Nia (NEE-ah) — purpose
Nia is studied on the fifth day. A good purpose is to try to be the best that we can be, and to help make our community great, too.

Kuumba (koo-OOM-bah) — creativity
Kuumba is celebrated on the sixth day. Kuumba means making or doing something in our own, unique way.

Imani (ee-MAH-nee) — faith
On the seventh day of Kwanzaa, Imani is practiced. We can show faith by believing in ourselves as well as in other people.

A is for AFRICA

Africa is the second largest continent. It has many countries. African Americans' ancestors came from Africa. Kwanzaa is a holiday that celebrates the rich heritage of Africa.

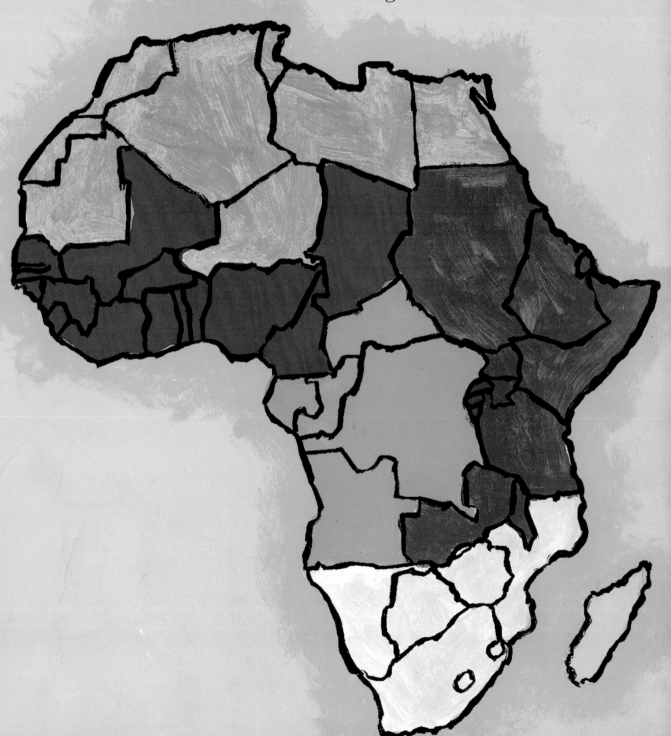

B is for BENDERA

The bendera (behn-DEH-rah) is the
African-American flag that is displayed
during Kwanzaa. It has three colors:
black represents African-American
people; red symbolizes their struggles;
and green stands for a happy future.

C is for CANDLE

A candle is a solid piece of wax with a string or wick inside that is burned to make light. Kwanzaa candles are called mishumaa saba (mee-shoo-MAH SAH-bah). They are the same colors as the bendera.

D is for DASHIKI

A dashiki (dah-SHEE-kee) is a loose-fitting shirt worn by people throughout Africa. Many African Americans wear dashikis during Kwanzaa to represent African pride.

E is for EMBE

Embe (em-beh) is a mango, a fruit that grows in many parts of Africa. Mangos are a part of some Kwanzaa dishes or are eaten alone as a sweet treat.

F is for FEAST

A feast is a large meal shared by many people. On the last day of Kwanzaa, family and friends get together for a feast called the karamu (kah-RAH-moo).

G is for GELE

A gele (gay-leh) is a long, narrow strip of cloth that African women and girls wear wrapped around their heads. Wearing a gele shows pride in African heritage.

H is for HARVEST

A harvest is a ripened crop of fruits and vegetables that is gathered at the end of the growing season. Many African villages celebrate and give thanks for their harvest each year. Kwanzaa comes from the African harvest celebration.

I is for INDIGO

Indigo is a blue powder made from the indigo plant. In many areas of Africa, it is mixed with water and used to dye cloth. To celebrate Kwanzaa, we can dye pieces of cloth to honor this custom.

J is for JEWELRY

Ornaments such as bracelets, rings, earrings, and necklaces are jewelry. Made from precious gems and metals, or beads, shells, and string, beautiful jewelry is an important part of dressing in many African cultures. Making simple bracelets or necklaces as Kwanzaa gifts is a way to practice creativity (Kuumba).

K is for KWANZAA, and also for KINARA

The kinara (kee-NAH-rah) is the wooden candleholder that holds the seven Kwanzaa candles. The black candle is placed in the middle, the red candles to the left, and the green ones to the right. The black candle is lit on the first night of Kwanzaa. On each of the following nights, one more candle is lit: first a red one, then a green one, then a red one, and so on.

L is for LAPA

A lapa (LAH-pah) is a broad piece of cloth that African women and girls wear wrapped around their bodies like a skirt. Lapas are popular African-style clothing worn at Kwanzaa time.

M is for MKEKA

The mkeka (em-KE-kah) is a special mat that is set on the Kwanzaa table. The kinara and mazao (mah-ZAH-oo), fruits and vegetables symbolizing the harvest, are placed on the mkeka.

N is for NEIGHBORHOOD

A neighborhood is a small part of the community that we live in. Kwanzaa teaches us to respect our neighborhood and to work together to make it a better place.

O is for OWARE

Oware (oh-WAH-reh) is an African game played with marbles or small stones. It is also called mancala (mahn-CAH-lah). Playing games together is a fun way to show unity and cooperation during Kwanzaa.

P is for **PLANTS**

Plants grow in the earth from seeds. Some plants provide us with fruits and vegetables. After harvesting the crops in Africa, it is time to plant new seeds. At Kwanzaa time, plan a small garden, indoors or out, to welcome in the new year.

Q is for QUILT

A quilt is a bedcover stitched together from many small pieces of fabric. Create a Kwanzaa quilt with African fabrics and family items that have some special meaning.

R is for RAFFIA

Raffia is a fiber that comes from the leaves of certain African palm trees. Raffia is used to make masks or to weave baskets, bags, and mkeka mats.

S is for SHAKERE

A shakere (shah-KE-re) is a rhythm instrument made from a dry, hollow gourd that is strung with beads. It is played for African dances and ceremonies and at Kwanzaa celebrations.

T is for TALES

Tales are stories that can be true or make-believe. Reading or telling African tales such as Anansi stories is a popular Kwanzaa activity.

U is for UJAMAA

Ujamaa, one of the seven principles of Kwanzaa, means cooperative economics. At an Ujamaa market, we can buy African or African-American products such as kente cloth, jewelry, and food.

V is for VIBUNZI

Vibunzi (vee-BOON-zee) is another word for muhindi (moo-HIN-dee), which are the dried ears of corn placed on the mkeka. Corn is a very important Kwanzaa symbol. Corn represents children, who are the future of a family.

W is for WATER

Water is a clear, natural liquid. It is a symbol of purity in many countries. During Kwanzaa, water is poured into the unity cup, the kikombe cha umoja (kee-KOM-beh chah oo-MOH-jah), and everyone drinks a special toast to the ancestors.

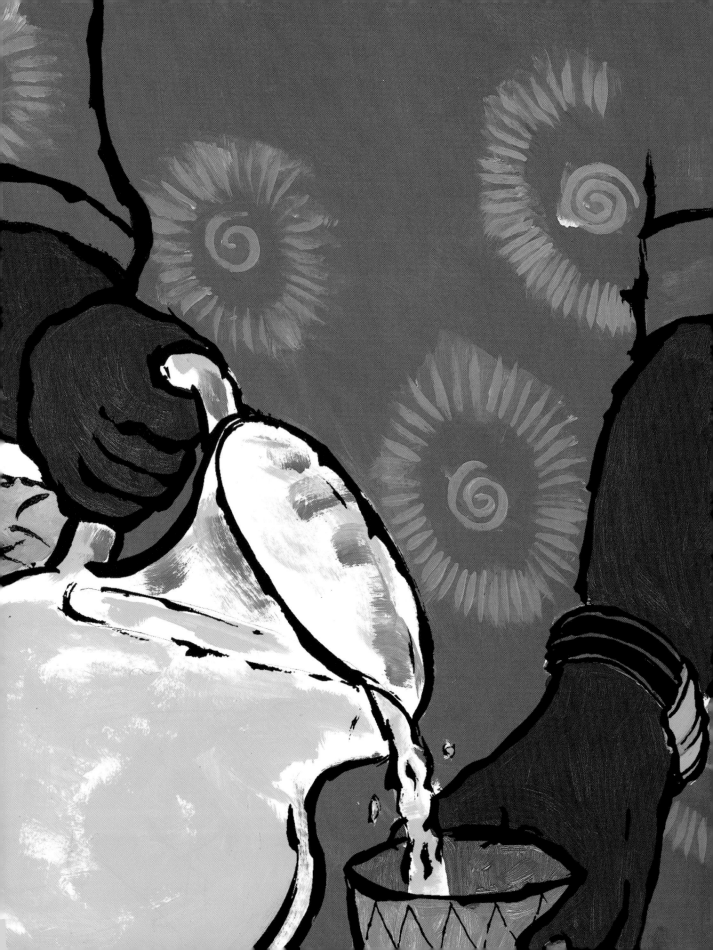

X is for XYLOPHONE

A xylophone is a musical instrument with bars that are struck to make sounds. Some xylophones are made from wood. They are used in song and dance in some homes at Kwanzaa time.

Y is for YAMS

Yams are vegetables similar to potatoes. They are an important part of the African diet. Yams and other vegetables are eaten at the karamu feast.

Z is for ZAWADI

Zawadi (zah-WAH-dee) means gifts. Simple gifts exchanged at Kwanzaa should be educational, cultural, or related to family values. Handmade items such as cornhusk dolls, wooden cars, and quilts make special gifts. Books and games are great gifts, too.